False Memories of a Cape Cod Clam Shack

JOEL HUSCHLE

LOS ANGELES † NEW YORK † LONDON † MELBOURNE

False Memories of a Cape Cod Clam Shack by Joel Huschle

ISBN: 978-1-947240-26-1
eISBN: 978-1-947240-27-8

Copyright © 2021 Joel Huschle. All rights reserved.

First Printing 2021

For information:

Bamboo Dart Press
chapbooks@bamboodartpress.com

Curated and operated by Dennis Callaci and Mark Givens

Bamboo Dart Press 011

www.pelekinesis.com

www.bamboodartpress.com

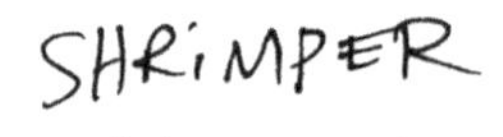

www.shrimperrecords.com

For all of my future surgeons and their horrible families.

Section One

Transaction Build 04.271 9
Joist Feathering 10
Vast Compounding 11
Earthen Passageway 12
Thwartage Fetch Scenario 2.874 13
after what seemed like four long years 14
Cough Vector Bacterium Intersect 2.702 15
Rate Kerning 426.882.01 16
Taking On Water 17
Taking on Water, Phase Two 18
Kufra Basin Aquifers and Dr. Joe Gannon's Destructive Influence 19
What's With Vinnie? A Comic Exploration of the Driving Forces that, um, Drive Human Behavior 20
Reservoir of Hurt 22
Taking on Water: Phase Three 23
The First Meeting of the Meritocracy of Witch-Babies at the Center of the Earth 24
Vincent: When Irish Eyes are Smiling 26
Tripoli 1951: King Idris and the Irish Estrogen Coverup 28
Professional Writer Colony Collapse 30
Taking on Water: The Lowrance Mark-5X Pro Fishfinder Mono 83/200 kHz 31

Sherry's Black Magic Sandwich 33
Trout of Souls 35
Reservoir of Hurt: The Rage is Genuine 36
Admiral Plotts Is Pretty Bad Ass 38
On Being a Head in a Bag: Dagmar's Head, Specifically . . . 40
Dance Routine (Practice Makes Perfect) 41

Section Two

praying haiku 44
Water Trap 46
I Drink Too Much 47
Remember 48
Secure Cabin 49
Singled Out 50
I'm Nothing 51
Constant Hurt 52
I got a dui 53
That's Not Music 54
Forbidder 55
Negotiations 56
Missile and Grain 57
Myths of the Empath 58

Appendix

61. Real Sensitivity
61. Arbitration
61. Kevin and the Horrible Headache
62. Enter Parents
62. Funny Farmer
63. Furniture Store
63. The Crucifixion of Mr. Finicky
63. Party Dress
64. Locus of Control
64. Thrush
64. I've Got Your Nose
65. Dairy Fire
65. Debts With Corsicans
66. Riboflavin
66. Imagine Dating
67. Comfort is Stagnation
67. Lime
68. Orange
68. Looking for your Foot
68. Nation of Friends
68. Zero Coupon Bonds
69. I've Often Thought About Your Remaining Eye
69. Lonely After Dinner
70. Maximize Your Profits in a Tax-Sheltered Investment
70. Jesus Christ
71. Child Killer
71. Terror Song
72. I'm Not Franklin
72. Instantly Person
73. I Built a Woman
73. Battle of the Network Stars
74. Hurting Words
74. Pam Dawber Potash Fantasy

Section One

Yell Hole?

Transaction Build 04.271

don't say flagrant
because if dumbsourcing is your bag
you've got it in the bag

I can't help that you got fired
and I didn't get you fired
but I might have tried
if I had known they would listen

Transaction Build 04.271 was a triumph
we think about your face
with an "X" through it

Joist Feathering

radiation from group 7
changed the mood at Manker Flats
heat passed from cold to hot that night
allowing the steel shapes of animals
a few unsanctioned moments
to feel alive in the harsh halogen glow

Vast Compounding

you talked up the plutocracy
and bought the pricey sliders
expensive tiny sandwiches
are best when they're insiders

November 18, 2011 at 7:28 AM

Make house key and PO Box key
Bring charger and Jake's card
Pharmacy
Dog food vitamins medications
Change message on work phone
Ask Bob to check on cats
Wash dog beds and crates
Coffee tea snacks sunglasses
Cash maps phone numbers

Earthen Passageway

the cave was a musty cave
littered with the skeletons
of NPR reporters
Lakshmi Singh was clutching a goblet
and Kai Ryssdal had an extra leg
the only light source was the tuning panel
of a Bang & Olufsen receiver
plugged in next to the blender

December 2, 2011 at 5:14 PM

Lettuce walnuts chamomile tea yogurt things other things lemons lime olive oil Doublehorn
Genius devil forms
Someone more soy milk
Steve coffee

Thwartage Fetch Scenario 2.874

we did not use zeroes as per your instruction
which made our nights at the lab a living hell
sure, we had some down time when we played "Yell Hole"
but we would always clean up and get back to work

January 12, 2012 at 11:31 PM
Old stringless shitty ears and a bad guitar

AFTER WHAT SEEMED LIKE FOUR LONG YEARS

(it was exactly four years straddling the millennium)
we submitted your proposal for review
and it was reviewed and rejected by the committee

now we find ourselves six years later
sharing a table at the Thwartage Fetch Conference in San Jose
and you are being hailed as a visionary
who could play a mean game of "Yell Hole"

February 17, 2012 at 12:15 AM

Bland Analytics

Data Yoursing is an applied metrics application based on the future use of words we already know about, including their order.

Cough Vector Bacterium Intersect 2.702

taking pills
is fun
I take pills
and have fun

let's take these pills
let's have some fun
I prefer these pills
manufactured with the patented process
of Cough Vector Bacterium Intersect 2.702
because pills manufactured with the patented process
of Cough Vector Bacterium Intersect 2.702
are more fun

June 23, 2012 at 2:39 PM
Pick pick pick
Convicinio

Rate Kerning 426.882.01

As we pull the numbers closer together
We end up with more space at either end
And even though we corral the data
They look better when left wild

May 2, 2013 at 5:13 PM
1st Saturday 10-12
Dick is unofficial manager.
8855

Taking On Water

the feelings and misgivings of the others around me
radiate out in waves
and rather than push through my permeated covering
they stop just outside of me
and wait

from anger ghosts and trust ghouls
love wisps and sorrow flies
they wait because there is no more room in me
and there will be no vacancies any time soon

January 11, 2016 at 3:48 PM

In the church of the lower abdomen there are bishops with certain Accu men
The pews are cushioned and the wine is real this little church has a lot of appeal

Taking on Water, Phase Two

I push a shopping cart full of groceries
Into a crematorium
There is a woman wearing oversized goggles
That extend into a white draped hood
Her gloves are thick like phonemen used to wear
And she does the thing I hate the most
She tries to help by grabbing one side of the cart and guiding it
As if I lack the ability to steer a fucking shopping cart
I tell her to let go and she refuses, saying "This is my crematorium."

So now I have an overly gloved goggle-faced inverse Darth Vader lady
Trying to pull MY shopping cart full of MY groceries
Toward the first of three industrial-sized ovens
I take a moment to notice the strength of goggle-lady's grip on the cart
And realize she is pulling the cart
Toward the opening door of the first oven
As I struggle and lose my grip
I know that none of these products will survive
Once they are in the oven
She wins the battle and we both watch the immolation
Through the smoky glass window of oven #1
Once it is finished I turn to leave and nod a slow and deliberate "yes"
When she instructs me to return tomorrow

Kufra Basin Aquifers and Dr. Joe Gannon's Destructive Influence

I woke up this morning thinking I had lost my humanity
After a cup of coffee and some time to reflect
I came to the chilling realization
My humanity had remained intact
It permeates all I do and say and think
But for a brief moment this morning
Innocence and freedom seemed possible

January 20, 2016 at 8:18 AM
Cut it out of me
920-0526

What's With Vinnie? A Comic Exploration of the Driving Forces that, um, Drive Human Behavior

Vinnie's cough started out as a tickle at the back of his throat
His first reaction was to deny he was getting a cough
The next morning his throat was so sore and swollen
he couldn't swallow
The glands on his neck were Jerry Lewis puffy
Though his thoughts were foggy he was able to remember
why he was in Portugal
Vinnie stood from the bed and almost collapsed when his
fevered blood followed gravity's cues
And rushed downward like electricity to ground
He regained his balance and briefly envied the laws of physics
Before the world in front of him turned from colorless fireworks
to black fuzz
Vinnie knew he had died but was no longer welcomed
in the world of senses
His body was discovered two days later after the guests
across the hall
Complained of a smell they described as a cross between
rancid Parmesan
And cat farts
The hotel housekeeper rifled through his belongings before
alerting the authorities

She scored a couple one-hundred dollar bills
from his money belt
And a bottle of strange looking prescription pills
that caught the light
In such a way that it was impossible to discern
their true color
She looked at Vinnie with pity because she knew
he was not blameless for his death
Yet she felt kind of bad for him anyway
He wasn't a bad looker (other than being dead and
having a Jerry Lewis puff-neck)
She popped one of the vibrant, color-confused
pills in her mouth and swallowed it dry
As she walked down to the lobby she felt a tickle
at the back of her throat

July 31, 2016 at 9:21 PM

Cock devil
You're not my friends
Not on the level

Reservoir of Hurt

A woman (we'll call her Phyllis, because that's her name)
Worked in a small, windowless utility shack
Thirty meters up from the current shoreline
Of Puddingstone reservoir
Measuring the emotional responses of brown trout
To human facial expressions
Phyllis was in her late twenties and had been a theater major
So she prided herself on her range and control of her facial muscles
She had even taught herself to cry without hesitation
Tears of joy or sadness
It was the reason she was hired
By Pinnacle Armor Corporation
This particular morning
She had three moderately sized brown trout
Eye-level with her on what she called the "fish shelf"
And she was making her rage face
The carefully wired fish were connected to a series of computers
On the far wall
Their responses to her expressions being transmitted
To Pinnacle's chief science officer
Who his colleagues referred to as "The Dragon"

Taking on Water: Phase Three

The Port of Long Beach was finally visible again
The fires were mostly out and the 30,000 foot high column
  of dirt and ash
Had drifted and shared its contents with the inland counties
The landscape had changed as evidenced by a one mile radius
Circular glass-bottomed lagoon that now existed
Where piers, docks, and crane towers had been before
Container ships from China, Korea, and Oman floated
  several miles offshore
Lucky enough to have been outside of the blast radius
Admiral Platts handed his binoculars to the voluptuous caucasoid
  Libyan boy named Dagmar
And said, "Dagmar, the detonation was at or just below sea level
No air involvement based on the debris cloud and crater depth"
Dagmar began cleaning the binocular lenses
  with a corner of his blouse
And handing them back to Platts, stated, "You might as well
  put these away
You've seen enough to know it was one of yours"

August 13, 2016 at 8:26 PM

In the face of courage, choose a Dutch pancake. In the face of terror, choose courage and a pancake. In pancake face, choose Dutch courage. It lifts your features.

The First Meeting of the Meritocracy of Witch-Babies at the Center of the Earth

Eleven was the fourth witch-baby to chew through half the planet
to arrive in the vast and undeveloped underground refuge
Three, who was almost fourth, awaited Eleven's initial proclamation
at the Equicratic Convention Hall
Numerous others (about 84 in all) were in attendance, but their back
stories (let alone their names) have not yet been thought out
Eleven approached the podium, wearing the the traditional black
onesie and a black pointed hat
Clearing his throat, he began singing:
Witch-Baby at the Center of the Earth Meritocracy Anthem
Our mothers were pregnant witches
Who gave birth in various boats
To throw us in the water
So we could sink to the bottom of the water containment system
(Whether it be natural, like a lake or ocean
Or artificial, like a reservoir or the Los Angeles River
Or what happened to poor Seven with the Pomona YMCA pool)
And chew our way here to our new home to form a true meritocracy
Knowing that our mothers were witches
Most have been killed or worse
But their sacrifice was worth it
Because look at our home

It's pretty nice
And you can't beat a meritocracy
Eleven finished and hastily exited the stage
His bluetooth earpiece had transmitted a message that could change everything
The voice was familiar because he knew who it was (by recognizing the sound)
The message was, "Admiral Platts was valuable. Long Beach is Secure. Dagmar out."

August 13, 2016 at 9:08 PM

Haiku Sweet Dreams
Do they have a plan?
Are you friends with a white witch?
They'll think you just drowned

Vincent: When Irish Eyes are Smiling

The lobby of Pinewood's main campus had Vincent confused
Instead of a quasi-sterile, brightly lit room with chrome-framed vinyl seating
And a doe-eyed receptionist who knew how to do the smile/head-tilt trick
He felt he was in the lobby of a roadside hotel
There were two battered couches
Of which one was occupied by a seemingly ancient labrador retriever
Who acknowledged Vincent's presence with a single eye opening
And then closing again
The "receptionist" was a thin adolescent male with red hair
And an unseemly mass of freckles that left only small hints of pale skin
Visible on his face and hands
Vincent approached Freckle-boy
Who was standing behind a wooden lectern
"Am I in the right place?" asked Vincent
Instead of answering the question
Freckle-boy yelled over to the dog, "Raymond!"
Raymond the labrador lifted his head and turned his whitened muzzle toward Vincent

Freckle-boy continued, "Raymond, demonstrate to Vinnie here that he's in the right place"

Vincent told the boy, "I prefer Vincent. Please don't call me Vinnie."

Raymond slowly and arthritically got off the couch and approached Vincent

Stopping about three feet in front of him and stated in clear, regional brogue

"You're Vinnie from now on. And you are definitely in the right place"

Freckle-boy laughed and gave Vinnie's shoulder a welcoming slap

And had Vinnie been dreaming he would have hoped the slap would awaken him

But here he was

Wide awake in a beat-up room with Freckle-boy and a talking dog

---

Haiku Arm Boy

Maybe I should go
What's fucking wrong with your arms?
Can't leave, laugh, love, live

TRIPOLI 1951: KING IDRIS AND THE IRISH ESTROGEN COVERUP

The new king loved the taste of dates
Which got him to wondering why the shape of an average date
Along with the placement of the date in his mouth
Would trigger within him uncomfortable feelings
He would wriggle out the pit with his tongue
And imagine he was free to dance with the men around him
He pictured the exhausted group shedding their
 sweat-soaked garments
And then fucking each other a whole bunch

These thoughts drove the new king bananas
So he devised a plan to change the masculine nature of the fruit
 of the date palm
By having an Irish pharmaceutical company
Pump tens of thousands of gallons of cruelly-derived estrogen
Directly into the Kufra Basin Aquifer
King Idris believed that within a few years
He would be able to savor a plump and luscious date
And be free to think about politics and weather patterns
Instead of his fairly graphic homoerotic fantasies
The plan didn't work to change the fruit's effects
Which drove the king totally bananas

And he swore he would never again eat another date

His health had steadily deteriorated since being overthrown in 1969
He had kept his pledge to avoid eating dates
Until in 1983 while on his deathbed, the king called out to his nurse
"A date, please. I would like a date."
The stereotypically sexy female nurse smiled and wagged her index finger at him
And called him a "naughty boy"
The king died a short while later

August 29, 2016 at 9:28 PM
What did the biopsy say?
Biopsies can't talk

Professional Writer Colony Collapse

I am the professional writer of this blog
There has been a ripple of sorts that has interrupted my thoughts
The ripple is not related to the divers
How could it be?
I had a dream last night about Cuban flags
Being used as spring roll wrappers
And then I had to go back to 4th grade
To let Mrs. Kamm finish the salt statue of Warren Harding

April 26, 2017 at 2:07 PM
Broken
Getting broken
I am getting broken

Taking on Water: The Lowrance Mark-5X Pro Fishfinder Mono 83/200 kHz

I was impressed with the powerful yet simplified performance
Of the Lowrance Mark-5X Pro Fishfinder Mono 83/200 kHz

I had been given the Lowrance Mark-5X Pro Fishfinder Mono 83/200 kHz as a birthday present
Yet my birthday was six months ago
And I was not certain who had purchased it for me

It was delivered to my home last Friday while I was at work
Since I work from home, I was there when it was delivered
I received the delivery politely
Even though I was surprised that my boss allowed me to accept it during work hours

I am self-employed
But that does not mean my boss is any less of a dick than your boss

The birthday card in the box was one of the funny ones from Target
It had a cartoon elderly white geezer shaking his cane at a birthday cake
There were so many candles burning that the cake was an inferno
Indicating the white geezer was quite old
There was a thought bubble above the man's head that read:
I ought to just give up and burn to death

I opened the card and there was a handwritten message
on the left side

Written in a language I did not understand

And on the right side there was a printed "punchline"

Which I suppose was related to the elderly white man in an
existential crisis

It stated:

Happy Birthday! At least your cane is still stiff!

June 10, 2017 at 9:32 AM

Organic cucumbers. Organic strawberries. To bucket. Glue. And the damn filter for the shop vac. Tilapia. Chicken.

Sherry's Black Magic Sandwich

Unfamiliar with Jack's kitchen
Sherry had a bitch of a time finding ingredients
To construct a sandwich

Jack's refrigerator would not open for her
Because the biometric lock
Did not recognize her thumbprint

Sherry looked at her palm
Taking note that the wound had already healed
She glared at the refrigerator door and began to chant:
Samahac et famyolas Harrahya!
The refrigerator opened and the mustard, pickles, and deli meat
Floated of their own accord to the counter
Tomatoes and lettuce released themselves from their vegetable drawers and followed the other ingredients
Sherry turned to the the pantry now
Feeling as if every cell in her body held power and answers
She again chanted:
Samahac et famyolas Harrahya!

Jack felt clean and frisky as an alley cat after his shower
He entered the kitchen wearing only a towel around his waist
He saw Sherry yelling at his pantry

His friskiness subsided as he watched his sandwich components
Float through the air to the cutting board on the counter

Sherry was, herself, now floating a few inches above
the tile floor of the kitchen
Jack approached her and noted the blue glow her body was giving off
And stated, "Not too heavy on the mustard. I'll be in the living room"

June 18, 2017 at 8:02 PM

Your trauma coat is heavy
And covers your beauty almost thoroughly
There is no one person who can get through it
You are warm but you are not safe
And in your trauma coat you're always awake
You are hyper-aware
To the point that you're not there
All I see is that heavy outerwear
Is there even a person under there?

Trout of Souls

He didn't know if he had one name
Or many names
And he wondered why he was even able to think
He remembered the woman who would make faces at him
And the night she drunkenly snipped the thin wires
That had connected him to a massive data network
His access to so much information suddenly stopped
Leaving him alone in his own mind
The face woman had released him back into the reservoir
Which made very little sense to him
Since she had methodically pithed the others
Once her experiments were completed
He was safely out of range when the grenade exploded
And wouldn't even know what a grenade was
Except that the departing souls of the human divers
Had entered into him
He had access to their thoughts and could feel them struggle for purchase
But for now he would keep them subdued and separate from one another
Until he learned more about who they once were
And what parts he would keep for himself
And though he did not have a mirror
He was certain he was making "happy face"

Reservoir of Hurt: The Rage is Genuine

At today's meeting
Phyllis had the unique distinction of being the only person
To ever get kicked out of the Puddingstone Reservoir
    Dan Brown Book Club
Most of the other members (actually all of the other members)
Were brown trout who had lost their data integrity

The phone rang, interrupting her plan to announce
That there would be no more book club meetings
    at her workplace
And that her feelings were hurt by their unanimous
    vote against her
Phyllis picked up the phone and used her "answer word"
To acknowledge both receiving and accepting the call

Admiral Platts was just offshore in a rowboat
    when he made the call
The medals and accommodations on his M1941 Parsons jacket
Reflecting off the lake surface with the last bit of sunlight
    left in this day
The utility shack sat about 90 meters away from his position
He knew that contact had been made when he heard
    the "answer word"

Four pairs of hands (eight hands total) rested lightly on the rowboat's bottom

The admiral's phone conversation unheard by the four fully-suited hand owners

Helen's team had been ordered to stand down and provide surveillance data only

But Helen thought of orders as mere suggestions and often disregarded them

Which was the reason she had an unparalleled record of success with silencing traitors

Admiral Plotts Is Pretty Bad Ass

His love was using the code words
And, alone in his boat
He was alert, in love, and erect
But even these distractions
Were not enough to keep him from noticing
The microbubbles from beneath his boat
As if he had paused upon a passage of dark club soda
Keeping the binoculars still on his face
And the sat-phone against his ear
He pulled a frag grenade from his belt with his left hand
And pulled the pin with his teeth
He let the lever flap open
There was no panic while he counted
Four. Three. Two. One.
He dropped the frag casually from the side of the boat
  into the water
He knew that if he timed it incorrectly
He would likely be wounded or killed
But all worthy risk required sacrifice
Especially if there was the possibility of establishing
  a connection of particular import
That was why the admiral seemed immortal

And even after tonight
The stories of an entire Seal Team being neutralized
In a filthy San Gabriel Valley reservoir
Would resonate from intelligence portals
On all continents
And other parts of the planet
And the Admiral would calmly dock
And meet his love
While together they would unwire the trout, killing them
And fully destroy the altered fish bodies
Keeping themselves warmed
By a fire fueled by the books of Dan Brown

November 18, 2017 at 9:37 PM

Yucatan napkin
Absorb without shame my friend
You end your day moist

On Being a Head in a Bag: Dagmar's Head, Specifically

I no longer need my eyes to see
They've dried to the point
Of being useless to me
The fact that I'm thinking
Is neither blessing nor curse
The sackcloth I'm kept in
Isn't unlike a purse
I actually feel a sense of relief
Because I don't have to eat
And I don't have to breathe
I don't have to worry about paying my bills
Of laundering clothes or taking my pills
I've no sense of smell although surely I'm stinking
And I'm starting to hear what my captors are thinking

May 1, 2018 at 8:30 PM
I can't believe how shitty it feels to be left out of these amazing deals

Dance Routine (Practice Makes Perfect)

Phyllis and the Admiral had sex
Once they finished, they ate food and talked
They did not bother to clean the dishes
Both of them (not the dishes, even though there were two dishes)
(four dishes if you count the soupspoons)
(or one could just say two bowls and two soupspoons)
(but I am having difficulty now picturing the Admiral and Phyllis eating soup after their sex because soup is not really after-sex food like a sandwich or leftover Chinese food)
(in fact I look back at the first line and think I must be the most unromantic blogger ever)

So let's just get this done: Phyllis ends up telling the Admiral she had released one of the fish when she was drunk. They argue. The Admiral is madder than a mad bunch of crazy hornets! Oh no!
What's going to happen now?

October 24, 2018 at 5:23 AM
Antiquities thieves
Give us back
Our antiquities please

Welcome to
Puddingstone
Reservoir

Section Two

PRAYING HAIKU

sofa cushion dents
there where your elbows dug in
what were you doing?

what causes me pain?
achilles tendonitis
are you happy now?

your roommate is hot
except for the chittering
that drives me crazy

flustering for cash
your cardboard sign has errors
you are no coward

the city building
is right there in the center
the city center

their new chair arrived
they unboxed and sat on it
the sitty center

the shit he sent her
right after the proceedings
real pictures of God

who released the child?
it was a woman named Car
are you happy now?

freshly charged with fraud
the collapsing sense of time
a bailiff named Carl

jerking and lurching
the class action lawsuit claimed
looks like lawsuits claim

we need your feedback
how much did you weigh at birth?
minus the juices

skirt steak recipes
float around me like ticker tape
but with recipes

here I am so high
cannot stay here not for long
just how will I die?

fight night! two women
absolutism lecture
let's move to new york

Water Trap

We hit the links hard last week
When it was still August
You held your lofted club like a pro
And said to me from the rough
The only god we know
Is this lovable golfball

The water trap is full of golfballs
Lovable golfball gods, one and all

September 20, 2019 at 6:48 AM
I know that death is inevitable I find this food inedible

I Drink Too Much

Oh I drink too much
Of the alcohol
My drinks are medium
Big and small

I drink to the point where I feel bad
I don't want this line to rhyme with sad
If I drank a little less I would've had a better rhyme
But I drank too much to make a better rhyme

December 5, 2019 at 8:46 PM
I touch the heads of all I see and now I've got a felony

Remember

Leave sooner
Laugh liquid
Help each other
Judge their bread
Blenkenviss. Blenkenviss.

April 23, 2020 at 8:17 PM
Lemon Balmers
Clandestined pork ridge
Wide potato
Cuntin Covid coco broke fridge
With potato

Secure Cabin

We brought sufficient provisions
To our secure cabin
Enough to last for three months
Just like the website said

October 16, 2020 at 10:16 PM

The unarmed midwife brought the thing
She brought the thing
The unarmed midwife
She brought the motherfucking thing

Singled Out

Some are married
You're not
You're singled out
You don't have a spouse
Who you gonna leave your money to?
Who do you want to bury you?
Live alone
Die alone
Embrace the truth, but
Believe the doubt
You're singled out
Don't take this wrong
Don't take this wrong

I'm Nothing

I used to be something
Now I'm nothing
I used to rely on praise
For sacrificing myself
In so many ways
And I used to get paid
I used to get paid
I used to be something
Now I'm nothing
Was I robbed blind?
Am I out of my mind?
Or did my true damaged self
Finally rise up to shine?
I used to be something
Now I'm nothing

November 24, 2020 at 9:00 PM
The smell around here is yuck
Please send a refrigerated truck

Constant Hurt

Even without the external world
I have a constant hurt
That blankets every axon and dendrite
A myelin coating of cold doom
Acting well for others
I writhe in dull agony
Familiar dull agony
All respite seems false
The certainty of disbelief
Is soldered to my self
I have a constant hurt

December 1, 2020 at 5:25 PM
Wheat: Redacted
You authorized the transactions
Our records show
We do not return this verdict lightly
Wheat is redacted
You are unwanted and unlovable
When wheels are set
In motion at the dealership
Or the auction
Do you remember the auctions?
Wheat: Redacted

I got a dui

I like pumpkin pie
Not canned pumpkin pie
I got a dui
You wanna share my cuff?
Am I restrained enough?
I like pumpkin pie
I'm gonna call your bluff
You look like a cop
You are certainly a cop
I got a dui
I'm just starting to stop

That's Not Music

I used to believe in the power of song
The singer wasn't as wide as he was long
A radioactive spell to keep you at arm's length
Some call it a weakness but that just makes it stronger
I couldn't get more Ray Dung Chonger
And gravity won't matter much longer
That's not music
It's a grey matter square
That's a reclition
From so far away

Forbidder

Wolf Blitzer Cogentin discontinued
W. Blitzer placed in 5-pt leather restraints
Suppine
One hundred of Vistaril seems big
W. Blitz has the ass of a god

Negotiations

The negotiations are not going well, as my attorney is embalmed (not dead) and staying in a Dodge Caravan in Cudahy. If you've never been to Cudahy, you'll notice nothing of Cudahy unless tricked into watching Cudahy videos on Carl Reiner's (barely functioning) 3rd Generation iPod found at the base of the last known chocolate plant in California.

Missile and Grain

Missile and grain
To send overseas
Both are the same thing
Send them overseas
Missile and grain overseas
Send the same thing overseas
Emit a low sigh for material fissile
Breathe back in to mask the pain
Missile and grain

Myths of the Empath

Your thoughts on narcissism are very one-sided And you've put a lot of thought into the term "gaslighted" Now I'm not saying that you're flawed in your dictum But sitting on a spear can put a tear in your rectum Myths of the empath Seep up from the depths

burn my things put me in jail shoot me in the face i don't care

kill my friends take my clothes cut me into thirds punch me in the nose

myths of the empath

pull my hair off stab my hands empty my savings squat on my land disparage my acquaintances thwart my goals

poison my doctors punch me in the nose

myths of the empath

Appendix

Real Sensitivity

If I could paint a picture of my insides as they are
You'd see a pretty picture like a bus ride there you are
You always take the bus
What's the matter with my car?

Arbitration

You were never alive
We were fooled, yeah!
We thought we saw you dancing
Cheek to cheek with Fidel Ramos
We thought you voted Republican
And bounced a lot of checks
You really showed Fidel how to dip and twirl
Put five dollars into his hat

Kevin and the Horrible Headache

Love is the souffle
Indifference is the cake
Kevin and the Horrible Headache
Words may carry messages
Of fish across the lake
I've only seen Kevin once
But man was he hurtin'
Had this big ol' head
Just a beatin' like a fresh heart
Fresh heart / don't start
You must think you're really smart
You am / you is / you are / you aren't
Don't upset apple Descartes

Kevin had a treehouse
Where his brother was indicted in a rape
Kevin and the horrible headache

Enter Parents

Enter parents
Common sense
You'll have to put your heart and feelings in the lawn
A showroom beauty
A little cutie
And when your father gets ahold of her she's gone
The interior of the Samsonite Traveleur
Feels cold upon your face
Enter parents
A little nonsense
Fidel Ramos would have smiled
To see you frown
She is so pretty
So itty bitty
We know that smiles are just a sad face upside down

Funny Farmer

It's not a powerful song
It's not a good song
It's not a rock and roll song
It's not a sad song
It's not a long song
This won't be played on the radio
We don't like you
We're not like you

Furniture Store

Never thought I'd make it
Never ever thought
Forced into surgery
Arrested for perjury
I don't like Freddie Mercury
Even though he was probably
A district court judge
In a dream I had when I was twelve
About a furniture store

The Crucifixion of Mr. Finicky

I watched them drag Mr. Finicky from his travel trailer
They worked huge steel Frisbees under his ribs
And I heard pop music in the background
Songs I remember from when I was a boy
Pop music was coming from the background
It was terrific to hear those songs again
It was refreshing just to hear those songs again

Party Dress

Baby I'm so sad I cry myself to sleep
Sometimes it gets so bad I just can't eat
My vision blurs and I can't stand
And you're not even there to hold my hand
It's all your fault I'm such a mess
Because you've been wearing your party dress
Your clinging dress is hugging every curve
It can't hide all the good things I deserve
It's tight and small and looks so frail
In certain states you'd go to jail
And since you're not with me
I think I'll have myself another drink

You enter the bar and all the men just stare
They're looking at that dress that's hardly there
My jealous heart then starts to twitch
And my big ol' boner starts to itch
And if I could only make one wish
I'd wish your dress was pudding
Butterscotch pudding with little maggots in it
I want your dress to disgust you
I want your dress to confuse you
I wish I had your dress
I want to be confused about myself
I want to be disgusted with myself

Locus of Control

We thought it was a bug
We were pretty funny
It's easy to be funny
When you don't have a child

Thrush

Stuck with thrush
Kid's stuff
Had enough
It's burning up
Hoof and mouth
My mouth
Spare mouth
My mouth

I've Got Your Nose

If I were to wave my hand over your face
You'd be the last one to know
You'd have two eyes and two ears and one mouth

But I'd be the one with your nose
I've got your nose
You couldn't smell the danger
Your double-barreled flesh-ball
Now belongs to a stranger
I've got your nose
I pulled it from your head
It would've been tragic
If I had grabbed your eyes instead
I'd have your eyes
You'd have your nose

Dairy Fire

My papa was a god fearin' man of the land
When I was growing up he used to burn my hand
He said it was to teach me 'bout the flames of hell
I knew that he would kill me if I ever did tell
My mama was a god-fearing woman of the world
She used to dress me up like a pretty little girl
She said it was to teach me how to be a good wife
So I could please my papa after mama took her life
Dairy fire, it's a man's desire
This road through life's a long one
And I know that I am tired

Debts With Corsicans

It was probably you
Settling old debts with the Corsicans
It took me ten years to find you
It took me one hour to feed your wife
I fed her tomatoes and grapes
And lightly browned crepes
If you could only have seen

The fresh salad greens
And the crispy croutons
And the batter fried prawns
It was a meal to remember
And a night to forget
And I'll never believe that you settled your debt

Riboflavin

Grandma Huschle used to say that if I ate the oats
They'd stick to my ribs
Well that scared me
So I got to thinking
What if my ribs were covered in oil
And came right off like aluminum foil
On a TV dinner
I would send my bones to get you
I would send my bones to fetch you up

Imagine Dating

Imagine dating
Imagine walking on the beach and holding hands
Imagine dressing up
Don't be late or you could spoil the dinner plans
Imagine kissing
Moist caresses of your lips against her neck
Should you try it?
You only live once so go for it
What the heck
Then suddenly she submits to soft entanglements of fuzz
There is confusion
Because your hand no longer now is where it was
You gaze into her eyes
They are beautiful

And she opens up her mouth
And it's all full of flies and bugs
And you yell "Aaagh"

Comfort is Stagnation

Frustration, titration
I'm going to join the National Guard
Protect the country by dressing frumpy
It really won't be that hard
I'll wear green
You'll be queen
When we kiss
It's obscene
I could love you every day for evermore
When we dance
I'm entranced
I will always be your man
Stay with me
You will see
Rabid horses by the tree
See their bodies stiff and rolling in the sun

Lime

You've been causing problems down in Lime
Now you're out on bail and you look fine
Let's take a little walk to the Honey House
We'll trap the cat and be the mouse
I heard you found a husband down in Lime
I guess that makes it four
Or is it five?
Those numbers never did matter none
Because you and me add up to fun
I've got the key that opens up your rind

Your father said he knows and he don't mind
Indifferent to my tangy love
I'll always thank the lord above
Down in Lime
You're so fine

Orange

The three of us
Heading to Demon
You peel oranges
Sharing wedges with your father
You have to be extra careful
Not to drip juice on the Corinthian leather
Rome wasn't built in a day

Looking for your Foot

My country eyes well up
With frontier tears
My campfire songs
Bring sighs of sadness
Looking for your foot

Nation of Friends

I'm in a nation of friends
People doing things to help me
But I don't want help
I just want to buy weapons
And think about my mom

Zero Coupon Bonds

I bought some zero coupon bonds
I thought their relative safety and value
Made them hard to get along without

And now I see financial light
It's come to me it must be right
I think I'll take the first-class flight
And sleep without the pills tonight

I've Often Thought About Your Remaining Eye

One look
A singular look
Can tell so much about you
A cry
A dear to my heart cry
A right from the start cry
Tears keep falling and rain keeps dropping
I found you so familiar
You almost seemed like the old you
The one I knew before you
Open the door to my heart
I've often thought about your remaining eye
Pie in the sky

Lonely After Dinner

I've seen you hiding in the stairwell
Cramped into the dark
You never took me on that picnic
That you promised in the park
You have your body so well hidden
I know because I'm smart
Within every interaction
There are a number of obligations
I am petrified of numbers
Y=5 analogations
Within every interaction
There's a loser and a winner

So if you won't leave the stairwell
I'll be lonely after dinner

Maximize Your Profits in a Tax-Sheltered Investment

Let me tell you
If you start saving now
You won't have a worry in the world
You'll be swimmin in assets
But only if you follow my advice
Financial independence is the goal for which we strive
Without my information there's no point in being alive
Defer your compensation and boost your IRA
You're foolish if you don't max out your 401(k)
A 403(b)'s ok by me but watch out for that withdrawal fee
Now mutual funds are second to none
But only in the long term
Utilities are the place you want to be
If you've got the money to burn
Healthcare is a down right now
And Ginnie Maes are stagnant
And start right now in a college fund
If your true love is pregnant
The payoff's there if you watch and wait
And if you learn a little
Hey, that's great

Jesus Christ

I know when you sleep
You only dream of me
Because your arms are open wide
Just like Jesus Christ
Sometimes when you sleep
I slowly lift your shirt

I start to salivate
Oh, your breasts are great
Jesus Christ
Open wide
Breasts are great
Salivate

Child Killer

Look out kids!
He's a child killer
A man who kills children
You best be careful
Because he's loose in your building
Just like a made for TV movie
Looking for fun and feeling groovy
There's a child killer
Killing kids for fun
He's got a large nest egg
He's number one
He has an emerging market fund
He bought it from Fidelity
Earned 34% in a stagnant economy
There's a child killer
Who cares for his future
Though he kills children
He maintains social stature

Terror Song

Dad has a knife
He's stabbing his wife
Mom has a saw
She's sawing off her own jaw
Mom without jaw

Dad without wife
They're making awful plans
You'll get cancer in your hands
Terror song

I'm Not Franklin

This isn't part of the broadcast
The minivan has a new latch
There won't be flesh on the roadside
So what's the catch?
I'm not Franklin
I'm no good with words
I'm not Franklin
I've got my shoe on the wrong foot
My education is no good
I'm the youngest of five kids
And I'm not mad at what John did
I'm not Franklin[1]

Instantly Person

What could be worse than instantly person?
The plane fills with gas
Reach for the mask
Bobby Kennedy/Jack Lord
Oh my god
A thief got your purse now you're instantly person
It's easy to try on the tights with the Rayon
Bobby Soxers/Barbara Walters

---

1 These are the original lyrics, though in the recorded version the line, "I'm not afraid of arachnids" was used instead of "And I'm not mad at what John did" at the request of Franklin. The 2021 Franklin assured me that the 1993 Franklin is ok with publishing the original lyrics.

Oh my god
Bobby Kennedy/Jack Lord
Oh my god

I Built a Woman

I built a woman
I made her torso out of glass
I built a woman
Without any eyes
And even though I built her
She did harm to me
It made me sad
The woman I built was bad
I built a woman
I made her legs out of wood
The woman was bad
Not good

Battle of the Network Stars

You lied to me about Andy
You lied to me about Tim
I've got one little question
Are you gonna lie to me about him?
Not that you're being unfaithful
I don't mind the taste
It's just when I hold you deep in my arms
I picture his face on a stick
You lied to me about Ruben
You lied to me about Tom
You even lied to my mom
Not that you're being unfaithful
I don't mind the taste
It's just when I hold you deep in my arms

I picture his face on a stick
You told me lies about college
You told me lies about cars
Battle of the Network Stars

Hurting Words

I got the letter you sent/words
I got the phone call too
I read the sign on the freeway
I get words from you
Words that cause infection
They won't wash off my skin
If I were god I'd make words a sin
I saw the message you left
I got the phone call too
I read the tattoo on the freak
I get words from you

Pam Dawber Potash Fantasy

Church bus
Repair clinic
Divorced comedians/comics
False memory of a Cape Cod clam shack
Your surgeon skipped town
After the Neil Young tribute band
Failed to play any Neil Young songs
Ambien party dress
A falling out in Lakewood
Your Pam Dawber potash fantasy
We all hoard thoughts
We are thoughtful

About the Author

Joel Huschle lives with his wife and two dogs in Pomona, California. He continues to write, record, and play gigs as a member of Wckr Spgt and Furniture Huschle.

112 N. Harvard Ave. #65
Claremont, CA 91711

chapbooks@bamboodartpress.com
www.bamboodartpress.com

www.ingramcontent.com/pod-product-compliance
Lightning Source LLC
LaVergne TN
LVHW080333110826
845155LV00024B/153
9781947240261